Dedication

Moaz Safi Yousef al-Kasasbeh
May 29, 1988 – January 3, 2015

Also by Yatir Nitzany

Conversational Spanish Quick and Easy
....
Conversational French Quick and Easy
....
Conversational Italian Quick and Easy
....
Conversational Portuguese Quick and Easy
....
Conversational German Quick and Easy
....
Conversational Russian Quick and Easy
....
Conversational Hebrew Quick and Easy
....
Conversational Yiddish Quick and Easy
....
Conversational Arabic Quick and Easy
Palestinian Arabic
....
Conversational Arabic Quick and Easy
Lebanese Dialect
....
Conversational Arabic Quick and Easy
Egyptian Arabic
....
Conversational Arabic Quick and Easy
Jordanian Dialect
....
Conversational Arabic Quick and Easy
Emirati Dialect

Conversational
Arabic
Quick and Easy

TUNISIAN ARABIC

YATIR NITZANY

Foreword

About Myself

For many years I struggled to learn Spanish, and I still knew no more than about twenty words. Consequently, I was extremely frustrated. One day I stumbled upon this method as I was playing around with word combinations. Suddenly, I came to the realization that every language has a certain core group of words that are most commonly used and, simply by learning them, one could gain the ability to engage in quick and easy conversational Spanish.

I discovered which words those were, and I narrowed them down to three hundred and fifty that, once memorized, one could connect and create one's own sentences. The variations were and are *infinite*! By using this incredibly simple technique, I could converse at a proficient level and speak Spanish. Within a week, I astonished my Spanish-speaking friends with my newfound ability. The next semester I registered at my university for a Spanish language course, and I applied the same principles I had learned in that class (grammar, additional vocabulary, future and past tense, etc.) to those three hundred and fifty words I already had memorized, and immediately I felt as if I had grown wings and learned how to fly.

At the end of the semester, we took a class trip to San José, Costa Rica. I was like a fish in water, while the rest of my classmates were floundering and still struggling to converse. Throughout the following months, I again applied the same principle to other languages—French, Portuguese, Italian, and Arabic, all of which I now speak proficiently, thanks to this very simple technique.

This method is by far the fastest way to master quick and easy conversational language skills. There is no other technique that compares to my concept. It is effective, it worked for me, and it will work for you. Be consistent with my program, and you too will succeed the way I and many, many others have.

Contents

INTRODUCTION TO
THE PROGRAM

People often dream about learning a foreign language, but usually they never do it. Some feel that they just won't be able to do it while others believe that they don't have the time. Whatever your reason is, it's time to set that aside. With my new method, you will have enough time, and you will not fail. You will actually learn how to speak the fundamentals of the language—fluently in as little as a few days. Of course, you won't speak perfect Tunisian Arabic at first, but you will certainly gain significant proficiency. For example, if you travel to Tunisia, you will almost effortlessly be able engage in basic conversational communication with the locals in the present tense and you will no longer be intimidated by culture shock. It's time to relax. Learning a language is a valuable skill that connects people of multiple cultures around the world—and you now have the tools to join them.

How does my method work? I have taken twenty-seven of the most commonly used languages in the world and distilled from them the three hundred and fifty most frequently used words in any language. This process took three years of observation and research, and during that time, I determined which words I felt were most important for this method of basic conversational communication. In that time, I chose these words in such a way that they were structurally interrelated and that, when combined, form sentences. Thus, once you succeed in memorizing these words, you will be able to combine these words and form your own sentences. The words are spread over twenty pages. The words will also combine easily in sentences, for example, enabling you to ask simple questions, make basic statements, and obtain a rudimentary understanding of others' communications. I have also created Memorization Made Easy techniques for this program in order to help with the memorization of the vocabulary. Please see Reading and Pronunciation of Arabic accents in order to gain proficiency in the reading and pronunciation of the Arabic language prior to starting this program.

My book is mainly intended for basic present tense vocal communication, meaning anyone can easily use it to "get by" linguistically while visiting a foreign country without learning the entire language. With practice, you will be 100 percent understandable to native speakers, which is your aim. One disclaimer: this is not a grammar book, though it does address minute and essential grammar rules. Therefore, understanding complex sentences with obscure words in Arabic is beyond the scope of this book.

People who have tried this method have been successful, and by the time you finish this book, you will understand and be understood in basic conversational Arabic. This is the best basis to learn not only the Arabic language but any language. This is an entirely revolutionary, no-fail concept, and your ability to combine the pieces of the "language puzzle" together will come with great ease.

This is the best program that was ever designed to teach the reader how to become conversational. Other conversational programs will only teach you phrases. But this is the only program that will teach you how to create your own sentences for the purpose of becoming conversational.

TUNISIAN ARABIC DIALECT

Tunisia is a North African country bordering the Mediterranean Sea and Sahara Desert, and has an estimated 11.4 million inhabitants.

In Tunisia, a set of dialects of Maghrebi Arabic are spoken by eleven million speakers and are referred to as Tounsi, Tunisian or Derja that means "everyday language." This distinguishes the languages from the official Modern Standard Arabic (MSA).

Like other Maghrebi dialects, its vocabulary is mostly Arabic but with significant Berber and Latin inclusions. Tunisian merges into Algerian Arabic and Libyan Arabic at the borders of the country. Tunisian Arabic is mostly intelligible to speakers of other Maghrebi dialects but is hard to understand or is unintelligible for speakers of Middle Eastern Arabic. Its pronunciation, vocabulary and syntax are different enough from MSA and Classical Arabic to not be mutually intelligible with either of them. It also has many loanwords from French, Turkish, Italian, and Spanish.

There is much multilingualism within Tunisia, and Tunisians often mix Tunisian with French, English, Standard Arabic, or other languages in daily speech. There has been integration of new French and English words with Tunisian Arabic, notably in technical fields, or replacement of old French and Italian loan words with standard Arabic ones.

Tunisian Arabic is also closely related to Maltese, which is a separate language that descended from Tunisian and Siculo-Arabic.

Spoken in: Tunisia

MEMORIZATION MADE EASY

There is no doubt the three hundred and fifty words in my program are the required essentials in order to engage in quick and easy basic conversation in any foreign language. However, some people may experience difficulty in the memorization. For this reason, I created Memorization Made Easy. This memorization technique will make this program so simple and fun that it's unbelievable! I have spread the words over the following twenty pages. Each page contains a vocabulary table of ten to fifteen words. Below every vocabulary box, sentences are composed from the words on the page that you have just studied. This aids greatly in memorization. Once you succeed in memorizing the first page, then proceed to the second page. Upon completion of the second page, go back to the first and review. Then proceed to the third page. After memorizing the third, go back to the first and second and repeat. And so on. As you continue, begin to combine words and create your own sentences in your head. Every time you proceed to the following page, you will notice words from the previous pages will be present in those simple sentences as well, because repetition is one of the most crucial aspects in learning any foreign language. Upon completion of your twenty pages, *congratulations*, you have absorbed the required words and gained a basic, quick-and-easy proficiency and you should now be able to create your own sentences and say anything you wish in the Arabic language. This is a crash course in conversational Tunisian dialect, and it works!

ARABIC PRONUNCIATIONS

PLEASE MASTER THE FOLLOWING PAGE IN ARABIC PRONUNCIATIONS PRIOR TO STARTING THE PROGRAM

Kha . For Middle Eastern languages including Arabic, Hebrew, Farsi, Pashto, Urdu, Hindi, etc., and also German, to properly pronounce the kh or ch is essential, for example, *Khaled* (a Muslim name) or *Chanukah* (a Jewish holiday) or *Nacht* ("night" in German). The best way to describe kh or ch is to say "ka" or "ha" while at the same time putting your tongue at the back of your throat and blowing air. It's pronounced similarly to the sound that you make when clearing your throat. Please remember this whenever you come across any word containing a kh in this program.

Ghayin . The Arabic *gh* is equivalent to the "g" in English, but its pronunciation more closely resembles the French "r," rather than "g." Pronounce it at the back of your throat. The sound is equivalent to what you would make when gargling water. Gha is pronounced more as "rha," rather than as "ga." *Ghada* is pronounced as "rhada." In this program, the symbol for ghayin is gh, so keep your eyes peeled.

Aayin is pronounced as *a'a*, pronounced deep at the back of your throat. Rather similar to the sound one would make when gagging. In the program, the symbol for *aayin* is *a'a, u'u, o'o,* or *i'i.*

Ha is pronounced as "ha." Pronunciation takes place deep at the back of your throat, and for correct pronunciation, one must constrict the back of the throat and exhale air while simultaneously saying "ha." In the program, this strong h ("ha") is emphasized whenever *ha, ah, hi, he,* or *hu* is encountered.

NOTE TO THE READER

The purpose of this book is merely to enable you to communicate in Tunisian Arabic. In the program itself (pages 17-38) you may notice that the composition of some of those sentences might sound rather clumsy. This is intentional. These sentences were formulated in a specific way to serve two purposes: to facilitate the easy memorization of the vocabulary and to teach you how to combine the words in order to form your own sentences for quick and easy communication, rather than making complete literal sense in the English language. So keep in mind that this is not a phrase book!

As the title suggests, the sole purpose of this program is for conversational use only. It is based on the mirror translation technique. These sentences, as well as the translations are not incorrect, just a little clumsy. Latin languages, Semitic languages, and Anglo-Germanic languages, as well as a few others, are compatible with the mirror translation technique.

Many users say that this method surpasses any other known language learning technique that is currently out there on the market. Just stick with the program and you will achieve wonders!

Again, I wish to stress this program is by no means, shape, or form a phrase book! The sole purpose of this book is to give you a fundamental platform to enable you to connect certain words to become conversational. Please also read the "Introduction" and the "About Me" section prior to commencing the program.

In order to succeed with my method, please start on the very first page of the program and fully master one page at a time prior to proceeding to the next. Otherwise, you will overwhelm yourself and fail. Please do not skip pages, nor start from the middle of the book.

It is a myth that certain people are born with the talent to learn a language, and this book disproves that myth. With this method, anyone can learn a foreign language as long as he or she follows these explicit directions:

* Memorize the vocabulary on each page

* Follow that memorization by using a notecard to cover the words you have just memorized and test yourself.

* Then read the sentences following that are created from the vocabulary bank that you just mastered.

* Once fully memorized, give yourself the green light to proceed to the next page.

Again, if you proceed to the following page without mastering the previous, you are guaranteed to gain nothing from this book. If you follow the prescribed steps, you will realize just how effective and simplistic this method is.

THE PROGRAM

Let's Begin! "Vocabulary" (Memorize the Vocabulary)

I, I am	Ena
With you	(Male/Female) M'aak
With him / with her	M'aah / m'aaha
With us	M'aana
For you	(M/F) Lik (read the footnote below)
Without him	Min ghiru (or 'blesh bih')
Without them	Min ghirhom (or 'blesh bihom')
Always	Dima
Was	Ken
This, this is, it's	(M) Hedha / (F) Hedhi
Today	Lyoom
Sometimes	Se'aat
Maybe	Yomkon
You, you are, are you?	(M)/(F)Inti
Better	Ahsen / khir / ahla
You (plural)	(M)/(F) Entom
He, he is	Howa
She, she is	Hiya
From	Min

Sentences from the vocabulary (now you can speak the sentences and connect the words)

This is for you
Hedha/Hedhi lik

I am from Tunisia
Ena min Tunes

Are you from Tunisia?
Enti min Tunes?

I am with you
Ena m'aak

Sometimes you are with us at the mall
Se'aat enti m'aana fil mall

I am always with her
Ena dima m'aaha

Are you without them today?
Inti min ghirhom lyoom?

Sometimes I am with him
Ena se'aat m'aah

*In Tunisian Arabic, there are gender rules. As of the second pronoun "you", saying for example "for you", it is the same regardless of the gender *Lik*. However, when referring to the third person, gender distinction comes into play, in which case "for him" translates to *Lih* and "for her" translates to "*liha*". However, if the sentence was "I did it for you" (i.e., I did this only because you are a special friend to me or because you mean a lot to me), here in this context we use *ala khatrek* either for a girl or a boy.

17

I was	Ena kont
To be	(M) Ykoon / (F) tkoon
The	El, l
Same / like *(as in similar)*	Nafs / kif
Good	(M) Behi / (F) Behya
Here	Hooni
Very	Barsha / yecer
And	W'
Between	Ma bin / bin
Now	Taw, tawa
Later / After / afterwards	Baa'diin/baa'd
If	I'tha / law
Yes	Ayh
To	L'
Tomorrow	Ghodwa
Person	Shakhs
Also / too / as well	Zeda / hatta *(read footnote)*

If it's between now and later
I'tha kein bin tawa w' baa'd
It's better tomorrow
Ghodwa khir / ahsen
This is good as well
(M) Hedha behi zeda (F) Hedhi behya zeda
To be the same person
(M) Ykoun nafs el shakhs / (F) tkoun nafs el shakhs
Yes, you are very good
(M) Ayh, inti behi barsha / (F) ayh, inti behya barsha
I was here with them
Ena kont hooni m'aahom
You and I
Inti w'ena
The same day
Nafs el-yoom

*In the Arabic language, adjectives usually proceed the noun. For example, "the same day" is *nafs el yom*. For example: "small house" / *dar sgheera*, "tall person" / *shakhs tweel*, "short person" / *shakhs k'seer*
There are exceptions, though. For example, when expressing admiration or something impressive, we can say, "How big is this house?" / *Ma akbarha hal dar?*
*In Tunisian Arabic there are two forms to signify "if" / *idha* and *law*. "If it's raining tomorrow, I am not going," for instance, in this case, we use "*idha.*" For "if I knew that th will happen, I wouldn't go to visit her," here the "if" is like "had I" and law will be used.
*In the Tunisian dialect, to express "too/also/as well" you use *hatta* at the beginning of the sentence. For example, "I love you too" / *Hatta ena nhebek*. You use *zeda* at the end of the sentence. "I love you too" / *Ena nhebek zeda*.
Behi in the Tunisian dialect has two connotations: 1) "Okay"/ "I agree"; and 2) "Good" "nice."

Me	Ni / li *(read footnote)*
Ok	Ayh/ ok / beh/ behi
Even if	Hatta law
No	La
Worse	Akhyeb
Where	Ween
Everything	Kol shay
Somewhere	Fi blasa ma
What	Shnou / shnowa
Almost	Takriban
There	Ghadi
I go	Nemshi

Afterwards is worse
Baa'diin akhyeb
Even if I go now
Hatta I'dha mshit taw
Where is everything?
Ween kol shay?
Maybe somewhere
Yomkon fi blasa ma
What? I am almost there
Shnou? ena takriban ghadi
Where are you?
Enti ween?

*In Arabic, the pronoun "me" has several definitions. In relation to verbs, it's *ni* or *li*. *Li* refers to any verb that relates to the action of doing something to someone, or for someone.
For example, "tell me," "tell (to) me" / (M/F) *kolli*.
Ni just means "me": "love me" / *heb'ni* or "see me" / *shoof'ni*
Other variations ([y]ya, i): on me" / *'aliyya*,"in me" / *fiyya*, "to me" / *liyya*, "with me" / *m'aaya*, "in front of me" / *koddemi*, "from me" / *minni*
The same rule applies for "him" and "her"—both become suffixes: –*o* and –*a*. Basically all verbs pertinent to males end with *o*, and all pertinent to female end with *a*.
"love her" / *nhebha*, "love him" / *nhebbu*, "love them" / *nhebhom*, "love us" / *nhebna*
Any verb that relates to doing something to someone, or for someone put l:
"tell her" / *kolha*, "tell him" / *kollu*, "tell them" / *kolhom*, "tell us" / *kolna*
Adding you as a suffix in Arabic is *ek* (2nd person)
"love you" / (M/F) *nhebbek*, "tell you" / (M/F) *nkollek*
*In Tunisian, for the first person you always use the prefix 'n' in the simple present tense, for example: *ena nhebbou / nhebha*.
*In the Tunisian dialect, the suffix "o" after a verb is intensified to *oo* (e.g., *Nhebboo* instead of *hebbo*).

House	Dar
In, at, at the	Fi
Car	Karhba
Already	Déja/ ça y est
Good morning	Sbeh el khir
How are you?	Shni ahwelek
Where are you from?	Inti mneen?
Impossible	Mostaheel /impossible
Hello	A'slema
What is your name?	Shesmek / shnou esmek
How old are you?	Kaddesh o'mrek?
Son	Weld
Daughter	Benet
To have	(M) A'ndou / (F) a'nd'ha / (Plur) a'nd'hom
Doesn't *or* **isn't**	Ma
Hard	S'iib (difficult)/ Yebes (solid)
Still	(M) Mazel / (F) Mazelet
Then (or "so")	Ya'ani / donc / I'dhan?

She doesn't have a car, so maybe she is still at the house?
hiyya ma 'a'nd'hesh karhba, ya'ani yomkon hiyya mazelet fil dar?
I am in the car already with your son and daughter
Ena déjà fil karhba m'aa weldek w bentek
Good morning, how are you today?
Sbeh el khir, shni ahwelek el-yoom?
Hello, what is your name?
A'slema, shnou esmek?
How old are you?
Kaddesh o'mrek?
This is very hard, but it's not impossible
Hedha s'iib barsha, ama moosh mostaheel
Then where are you from?
Ya'ani inti mneen?

*In Arabic, possessive pronouns become suffixes to the noun. For example, in the translation for "your," *ek* applies to both, the masculine and the feminine forms:
   "your book" / *ktebek*
   "your house" / *darek*
*In the Arabic language, as well as in other Semitic languages, the article "a" doesn't exist. "She doesn't have a car," *hiya ma a'nd'hesh karhna*.
*Tunisians use French as their second official language, therefore, several words from the French language are incorporated in their native dialect. There is no other form to signify "already", which Tunisians use, except for *déja / ça y est*. The Arabic translation for "impossible" is *mostaheel* however the French variation impossible is used more frequently.

Thank you	Shokran/ merci
For	Ala khater
Anything	Illi yji / ay haja
That, That is	(M) Hedha / (F) Hedhi
Time	Wakt
But	Ama / Lekin
No/ Not	La / ma/ moosh
I am not	Ena' manish
Away	B'eid
Late	Makhar
Similar, like	Yeshbah
Another/ Other	(M) Wehed ehker / ekher (F) wahda okhra / okhra
Side	Jnab / bah'dha/ sheera
Until	Hatta
Yesterday	Emis
Without us	Maghirna
Since	Min
Day	Nhar/yoom
Before	Kbal

Thanks for everything
Shokran ala kol shay
It's almost time
Sar el-wakt takriban
I am not here, I am away
Ena moosh hooni, ena b'eid
That is a similar house
Hedhi dar tshab'helha
I am from the other side
Ena min el-sheera l'okhra
But I was here until late yesterday
Lekin ena kont hooni el-wakt makhar emis
I am not at the other house
Ena moosh fil dar l'okhra

*In Tunisian Arabic, there are two separate cases used to signify "side": *bah'dha* and *sheera*. For "I am from the other side" *sheera*, but for "I stand by your side" here "your side" is *bah'dhek*.
*Negations are expressed as *la, ma,* and *moosh*
"No" / *la*
"I say no" / *Ena nkool la*
Negations preceding the verb are expressed as follows:
"I don't want" / *Ena ma nhebesh*
Expressing negation regarding non-verbs.
Moosh
"This isn't impossible" / *Hedha moosh mostaheel.*
"I am not here" / *Ena moosh hooni.*

I say / I am saying	Nkool / ena nkool
What time is it?	Kaddesh el-wakt taw
I want	Ena nheb
Without you	Min ghirek
Everywhere /wherever	Fil blayes el-kol / fi ay blasa
I am going	Nemshi
With	M'aa
My	Mte'ii (read footnote)
Cousin	(S)(M) Wled 'ammi, (F)benet 'ammi /(P) Wled 'ammti, bnet 'ammti
I need	Mohtej / hajti/ lezemni
Right now	Taw/tawa
Night	Leel
To see	Yshoof/ yraa
Light	Dhaw
Outside	El-barra
Without	Min ghir
Happy	Farhan
I see / I am seeing	Nshoof / ena nshoof

I am saying no / I say no
Ena nkool la / nkool la
I want to see this today
Nheb nshoof hedha lyoom
I am with you everywhere
Ena m'aak fil blayes lkol
I am happy without my cousins here
ena ferhan min ghir wled 'ammi hooni
I need to be there at night
Lezemni nkoon ghadi fil leel
I see light outside
Nshoof fi dhaw el-barra
What time is it right now?
Kaddesh el-wakt taw?

*"Mine" / mte'ii is a possessive pronoun. Mte'ii also means "my" but also becomes a suffi to a noun and it is placed only after a noun. Nouns ending in a vowel end with –ti. Noun ending with a consonant end with –i. For example:
"cousin" / weld 'amm, "my cousin" / weld 'ammi, "cup" / kess, "my cup" / kessi
For second and third person masculine noun, weld ("son"), male and female (S) ek, (P) kom. "His" – mte'oo/ "hers" – mte'ha, noun endings will be o (for male) and a (for female). "your son" / (m. and f.) weldek, "your (plural) son" / (m. and f.) wledkom, "his son" / weld "her son" / weld'ha, "our son" / weldna, "their son" / weld'hom
For second and third person feminine noun: "car" / karhba.
"your car" / karhabtek, "your (plural) car" / karhbetkom, "his car" / karhabto, "her car" / karhbet'ha,"our car" / karhbetna, "their car" / karhbet'hom

*This isn't a phrase book! The purpose of this book is solely to provide you with the tool to create your own sentences!

Place	Blasa
Easy	Sehel
To find	Yelka
To look for/to search	Ylawwej
Near / Close	Kreeb
To wait	Yestanna
To sell	Ybi'i
To use	Ystaa'mill
To know	Yaa'ref
To decide	Ykarrer
Between	Mabin
Both	Ezzouz
To	L'
Next to	Janb/ bahdha

This place it's easy to find

Hedhi blasa sehel besh telkaha

I want to look for this next to the car

Nheb nlawwej ala hedha bahdha el-karhba

I am saying to wait until tomorrow

Ena nkoul nistanew hatta l'ghodwa

This table is easy to sell

Hedhi tawla sehel besh tbii'ha

I want to use this

Nheb nista'mil hedhi (or hedha for m.)

I need to know where is the house

Nheb na'aref el-dar ween mawjouda

I want to decide between both places

Nheb nkkarer mabin ezzouz blayes

*Please pay close attention to the conjugation of verbs, whether they are in first person, second, or third. Unlike Anglo-Germanic languages, Latin languages, or even Classical Arabic, in which the first verb is conjugated and the following is always infinitive, in colloquial Arabic, it is quite different. The first verb is conjugated and the following one is conjugated as well. Keep in mind: The Tunisian dialect of the Arabic language is considered a colloquial, rather than an official language.

Because	Khater / 'ala-khater
To buy	Yeshri
Life	'Omr, hayet
Them, they, their	Lihom/ hooma/ mt'ehom
Bottle	Dabbouza
Book	Kteb
Mine	Lili/ liya/ mt'eii
To understand	Yefhem
Problem / Problems	(S) Moshkla/ (P) Mashekil
I do / I am doing	Naa'mel / ena naa'mel
Of	Mte'i
To look	Yshouf/ yraa
Myself	Ena
Enough	Yakfi / yezzi
Food / water	Mekla / ma
Each/ every/ entire/ all	El-kol / kolhom/ jm'ii
Hotel	Outil/ hotel

I like this hotel because I want to look at the beach
Y'ejbni hedha l outil khater nheb nshouf el-shatt
I want to buy a bottle of water
Nheb neshri dabbouza ma
I do this every day
Na'amel hedha kol yoom
Both of them have enough food
Ezouz 'anhdom mekla takfi
That is the book, and that book is mine
Hedha howa el-kteb, w hedha el-kteb mte'ii
I need to understand the problem
Ena lezimni nefhem el-moshkla
I see the view of the city from the hotel
Nshouf mandher el-mdina mil hotel
I do my homework today
Ena na'amil droosi lyoom
My entire life (all my life)
'Omri kemil

*There are two ways of saying "life" in Arabic: *'omr* and *hayet*.

I like	Nheeb/ ye'jebni
There is / There are	Famma
Family / Parents	'Ayla / waldin
Why	'Alesh
To say	Ykoul
Something	Haja
To go	Yemshi
Ready	Hadher
Soon	Kreeb / ala kreeb
To work	Yekhdem
Who	Shkoon / illi
Busy	Mashghool
That (conjunction)	(m) Anno / (f) anha
I Must	Lezem
Important	Mouhemma

I like to be at my house with my parents
Ena nheb nkoon fi dari m'aa waldiya
I want to know why I need to say something important
Nheb na'aref 'alesh lezimni nkool haja mouhemma
I am there with him
Ena ghadi m'aah
I am busy, but I need to be ready soon
Ena mashghool, ama lezimni nahdhar ala kreeb
I like to go to work
Nheb nemshi lel khedma
'Who is there?
Shkoon ghadi?
I want to know if they are here, because I want to go outside
Nheb na'aref hooma hooni walla, khater nheb nokhrej
There are seven dolls
Famma sab'aa lou'ab
I need to know that it is a good idea
Nheb na'aref anha fekra behya

*In the last sentence, we use "that" as a conjunction (*anha*).

How much /How many	Kaddesh
To bring	Yjeeb
With me	M'aaya
Instead	Fi 'oudh
Only	Kahaw/ kein
When	Wakt
I can / Can I?	Najjem / najjem?
Or	Aw/walla
Were	Kenoo
Without me	Maghiri / min ghiri
Fast	Fisaa'
Slow	Beshwaya
Cold	Bered
Inside	El-dekhil
To eat	Yekil
Hot	Skhoun
To Drive	Ysook

How much money do I need to bring with me?
Kaddesh floos lezimni njeeb m'aaya

Instead of this cake, I want that cake
Fi 'oudh hal gateau, nheb hal gateau

Only when you can
Kein wakt tnajjem

They were without me yesterday
Kenoo min ghiri ames

Do I need to drive the car fast or slow?
Lezimni nsook el-karhba fisaa' walla beshwaya

It is cold inside the library
Famma bard fi west lmaktba

Yes, I like to eat this hot for my lunch
Ayh, nheb neekil hedha skhoun fi ftouri

I can work today
Najjem nekhdem el-yoom

*"Were" is *kenoo*, "we were" is *konna*.

To answer	Yjeweb
To fly	Yteer / ysefer (read the footnote please)
Time / Times	Marra / Marrat
To travel	Ysefer
To learn	Yt'aallem
How	Kifesh
To swim	Y'oom
To practice	Yitmarren/ yetdarreb
To play	Yel'aab
To leave (something)	Ykhalli
Many /much /a lot	Barsha
I go to	Nemshi 'ala khater/besh
First	Awwel
To leave (a place)	Yemshi
Around	Hawl

I want to answer many questions
Nheb njeweb 'ala barsha as'ila
I must fly to Dubai today
Lezem nsafer el-Dubai lyoom
I need to learn how to swim at the pool
Lezemni nit'aalem kifesh n'oom fil piscine
I want to learn to play better tennis
Nheb nit'aalm nil'ab tennis ahsan
I want to leave this here for you when I go to travel the world
Nheb nkhalli hedha hooni leek wakt nemshi nsaefer hawl l'aalam
Since the first time
Min awwel marra
The children are yours
Esghar sgharek inti

*In Arabic there are 3 definitions for time:
-Time, *wakt* refers to; era, moment period, duration of time.
-Time(s), *marra*(t) refers to; occasion or frequency.
-Time, *se'aa* in reference to; hour, what time is it.
-* There are two forms of the word fly:
-"To fly" (like birds do) *yteer*;
-"To take flight" / *ysefer*.
*With the knowledge you've gained so far, now try to create *your own* sentences!

27

Nobody / Anyone	Hatta had / had
Against	Dhodd/ 'aks
Us	Ahna
To visit	Yzoor
Mom / Mother	Mama, ommi
To give	Yaa'ti
Which	Anehou / illi
To meet	Ykabel
Someone	Had
Just	Kahaw/juste
To walk	Yemshi
Week	Jom'aa
Towards	Bittijehh
Than	Min
Nothing	Hatta shay

Something is better than nothing
Haja khir min blesh
I am against him
Ena dhoddo
Is there anyone here?
Famma shkoun hoon?
We go to visit my family each week
Ahna nemshiw ntollo ala l'ayla kol jom'aa
I need to give you something
Nheb naa'tik haja
Do you want to go meet someone?
T'hebshi temshi tkabel hadd?
I was here on Wednesdays as well
Ena kont hooni nhar lerb'aa zeda
Do you do this everyday?
Inti taa'mel hakka kol yoom?
You need to walk around, but not towards the house
Inti lezmek taa'mel doora, ama moosh bittijeh el-dar

*In Arabic, when using the pronoun "you" as a direct and indirect object pronoun (the person who is actually affected by the action that is being carried out) in relation to a verb, the pronoun "you" becomes a suffix to that verb. That suffix becomes *ik* (masc.) *ek* (fem.). For example: "to give" / *yaa'ti*: "to give you" / *besh naa'tik*, "to tell" / *ykool*: "to tell you" / *besh nkollek* (m.), *qoolik* (f.), "to see" / *shoof*, "see you" / *yshoofek*: "to see you" (plural) / *nshoofkom* (m.), *shoofkan* (f.)
For third person male, add *o* and *om* for plural, for female add *ha* and *om* for plural. For example: "tell him" / *kollo*, "tell her" / *kolha*, "see them" / *shoofhom* (m.), *shoofhen* (f.), "see us "/ *shoofna*.
*There are two forms of the word "which" in Tunisian Arabic:
"Which one?" / *Anehou*
28"Which proves that" / *illi*

I have	'Andi
Don't	Ma
Friend	Saheb, sadeek
To borrow	Yetsallef
To look like / resemble	Yeshbah
Grandfather	Jaddi
To want	Yheb
To stay	Yok'od
To continue	Ykammill
That's why	Heka
Way	Kayyes/ sheraa'/ treek
I don't	Manish
To show	Yetfarrej
To prepare	Yhadher
I am not going	Ena manish meshi

Do you want to look like Salim?
Theb twalli tshabah Salim?
I want to borrow this book for my grandfather
Ena nheb nitsallef hedha el-kteb l'jaddi
I want to drive and to continue on this way to my house
Ena nheb nkammel nsook fi hedha el-treek hatta noosil lil dar
I have a friend there, that's why I want to stay in Sfax
'Andi saheb ghadi, heka alesh nheb nok'od fi Sfax
I am not going to see anyone here
Manish besh nshoof hatta had hooni
I need to show you how to prepare breakfast
Lezemni nwarrik kifesh t'hadhdher ftoor esbeh
Why don't you have the book?
Alesh ma 'andeksh el-kteb?
That is incorrect, I don't need the car today
Hedha ghalet, mahajtish bil karhba el-yoom

To remember	Yetfakker
Your	Mte'ik
Number	Rakm / noomru
Hour	Se'aa
Dark / darkness	Dhlam
About / on the	'La/ hawl/ fi
Grandmother	Jadti
Five	Khamsa
Minute / Minutes	Dkika/ dkayak
More	Akther
To think	Yfakker / ykhammem
To do	Yaa'mel
To come	Yji
To hear	Yesmaa'
Last	Ekher
To talk / To Speak	Yetkallam / yahki

You need to remember my number

Lezmek titfakker rakmi

This is the last hour of darkness

Hedhi ekher se'aa mte' dhlam

I want to come and to hear my grandmother speak Arabic

Ena nheb nji w nesmaa' jadti tahki bil 'arbi

I need to think more about this, and what to do

Nheb nfakker akther fil sujet hedha, w shnu naa'mel

From here to there, it's only five minutes

Min hooni l'ghadi, juste khamsa dkayak

The school on the mountain

El-madrsa fil jbal

*In Arabic with the question "is it?", the "it" can pertain to either a masculine or feminine noun. However, whenever pertaining to a masculine or feminine noun, it will become *howa* or *hiya*. For example, when referring to a feminine noun such as *karhba* ("the car"), "is it (the car in question) here?" / *hiya hooni?* When referring to a masculine noun such as *kalb* ("a dog"), "is it (the dog in question) on the table?" *howa ala tawla?* For neuter, it's *hedha*. However, I yet again wish to stress that this isn't a grammar book!

Early	Bekri
Tunisia	Tunes
Again	Marra okhra
Arabic	Arabi
To take	Yekhodh
To try	Yjarreb/ hawel
To rent	Yekri
Without her	Min ghirha
We are	Ahna
To turn off	Ytaffi/ ysakker
To ask	Yis'al/ yotlob
To stop	Ywakkef
Permission	Edhn
While	Fatra/zaman

He needs to leave and rent a house at the beach
Lezmo yemshi w yekri dar 'ala el-shatt
I want to take the test without her
Ena nheb nekhedh el-test min ghirha
We are here a long time
Ahna hooni min modda
I need to turn off the lights early tonight
Lezemni ntaffi el-dhawet bekri ellila
We want to stop here
Ahna lezemna nekfu hooni
We are from Sousse
Ahna min Sousse
The same building
Nafs el-banya
I want to ask permission to leave
Nheb notlob l'edhn besh nokhroj

To open	Yhell
A bit, a little, a little bit	Shwayya
To pay	Yidfaa'
Once again	Marra okhra
There isn't/ there aren't	Mafammesh
Sister	Okht
To hope	Yitmanna
To live (to exist)	Y'eesh
To live (in a place)	Yaskun
Nice to meet you	Tsharaft bmaa'reftek
Name	Ism
Last name	Lakab
To return	Yarjaa'
America	Amarica
Door	Beb

I need to open the door for my sister
Lezemni nhel el-beb l'okhti
I need to buy something
Lezemni neshri haja
I want to meet your sisters
Nheb nkabel okhtek
Nice to meet you, what is your name and your last name?
Tsharraft b maa'reftek, shnu el-esm w el-lakab mte'ik
To hope for a little better
Nitmanna shay ahsan
I want to return from the United States and to live in Qatar without problems
Nheb narjaa' min Amarica w nheb noskon fi Qatar maghir mashekill
Why are you sad right now?
(M)alesh mitghashesh tawa? (F) alesh mitghashesha tawa?
There aren't any people here
Mafamma hatta had hooni
There isn't enough time to go to Djebra today
Mafamesh wakt kefi besh temshi l'djerba lyoom

---

*In Tunisian Arabic, regarding the verb "to meet," there are two separate cases to define this verb: *tejtema'* and *kabil*, depending of the context. To meet for business is *tejtema'*. To meet for getting acquainted is *kabil*. In the sentence, "Do you want to go meet someone?" (the sister, getting acquainted with her), it's *kabil*.
*This *isn't* a phrase book! The purpose of this book is *solely* to provide you with the tools to create *your own* sentences!

32

To happen	Yseer
To order	Yotlob
To drink	Yeshrob
Excuse me	Samahni/ naa'tadhir
Child	(M) Ebn/ weld, (F) Bint
Woman	M'ra
To begin / To start	Yebda
To finish	Ykammel / yoofa
To help	Y'aawen
To smoke	Yetkayyef
To love	Yheb
Afternoon	El-kayla

This must happen today
Hedha lezem ysir el-yoom
Excuse me, my child is here as well
Samahni, weldi/benti hooni zeda
I love you
Ena nhebek
I see you
Nshoof fik
I need you at my side
Hajti bik m'aaya
I need to begin soon to be able to finish at 3 o'clock in the afternoon
Lezemni nebda ala kreeb besh najjem nkammel tletha mte' el-kayla
I need help
Hajti b'muse'ada
I don't want to smoke once again
Ma nhebesh netkayyef marra okhra
I want to learn how to speak Arabic
Nheb nit'aallem nahki bil 'arbi

*"To help" is 'aawen. However, "help!" is muse'ada. "I need help" or "I need rescue" /ena hajti b muse'ada.

To read	Yakra
To write	Yekteb
To teach	Y'aallem
To close	Ysakker
To choose	Yakhtar
To prefer	Yfadhal/ ykhayyar
To put	Yhott
Less	Akal
Sun	Shams
Month	Sh'har
I Talk	Nahki/netkallem
Exact	Shih / bil dhabt

I need this book to learn how to read and write in Arabic because I want to teach in Egypt
Hajti bel kteb hedha besh nit'aallem nakra w nekteb bil 'arbi khater nheb nkarri fi Masr

I want to close the door of the house
Lezemni nsakker beb el-dar

I prefer to put the gift here
Nkhayyer nhott el-hadiya hooni

I want to pay less than you for the dinner
Nheb nedfaa' akal mennek fil 'asha

I speak with the boy and the girl in French
Netkallem m'aa tfol wel tofla bel Français

There is sun outside today
Famma shams el-barra el-yoom

Is it possible to know the exact date?
Momken naa'ref el-date bil dhabt?

Where is the airport
Ween el-matar?

I need to go to sleep now
Lezemni nemshi norkod tawa

*"For the" is *l'*
*"In" is *bil*
*With the knowledge you've gained so far, now try to create your own sentences!

To exchange (*money*)	Ysarraf
To call	Yotlob
Brother	Khu
Dad	Bu
To sit	Yok'od
Together	M'aa b'adhna
To change	Ybaddel
Of course	Akeed / bien sur
Welcome	Ahla/ marhba
During	Wakt
Year/Years	(S)'Am/sna/(P)a'wem/sneen
Sky	Sma
Up	Fook
Down	Loota
Sorry	Samahni/naa'tadher
To follow	Ytabba' /yelhak
To the	Ila / lil / l'
Big	Kbeer
New	Jdeed
Never / ever	Abadan/marra okhra/jemla

I don't want to exchange this money at the bank
Ma nhebesh nsarraf hal floos fil banka
I want to call my brother and my dad today
Ena nheb nkallem khuya w buya lyoom
Of course I can come to the theater, and I want to sit together with you and with your sister
Akeed najjem nji lil masrah, w nheb nok'od bahdhek w bahdha okhtek
I need to go down to see your new house
Lezemni nahbat loota besh nshoof darek el-jdida
I can see the sky from the window
Najjem nshoof el-sma mil shobbeik
I am sorry, but he wants to follow her to the store
Naa'tadher, ama yheb ytabbaa'ha lil hanoot
I don't ever want to see you again
Ma nhebesh nshoofek marra okhra

*In Tunisian dialect, brother is *khu*, and dad is *bu*. However, "my dad" is *buya* and "my brother" is *khuya*. "My sister" is *okhti*, and "my mother" is *ommi*.
*For the possessive pronouns, her (*ha*) and him (*o*), both become suffixes to the verb or noun. Concerning nouns: her house / *darha*, his house / *daro*, concerning cases regarding verbs, please see footnotes on page 19.

To allow	Ykhalli
To believe	Ysaddak
Morning	Sbeh
Except	Bekhlef / appart
To promise	You'ed
Good night	Tisbah 'ala khir
Each	Kol
People	Ness / 'abed
To move (an object)	Yhawwel
To move (to a place)	Yhawwel
Far	B'eid
Different	Mokhtalef/ moosh kif/mbaddel
Man	Rajel
To enter	Yodkhol
To receive	Yestalam/ yekhodh/yekbel
Quickly	Fisa' fisa'
Good evening	Nharek zin / Bonsoir
Left / right	Y'sar / ymeen
Street	Kayyes/ nahj/ sheraa'

I need to allow him to go with us, he is a different man now
Lezemni nkhallih yemshi m'aana, howa taw rajel mokhtalef

I believe everything except this
Nsaddak kol shay bikhlef hedha

I promise to say good night to my parents each night
Noo'ed besh nkool tesbah 'ala khir l'waldiya kol lila

The people from Jordan are very pleasant
El-ness li mil Ordon behyeen barsha

I need to find another hotel very quickly
Lezmeni nilka hotel ekher fisa' fisa'

They need to receive a book for work
Lezemhom yestalmu kteb lil khedma

I see the sun in the morning
Nshoof el-shams fil sbeh

The house is on the right side of the street
El-dar 'ala ysar el-sheraa'

*There are two forms of the word "except"/ *bekhlef* and *appart*. *Appart* is the commonly used French variation.

36

To wish	Yetmanna
Bad	Mshoom/ khayeb
To Get	Yekhodh / yekhu
To forget	Yensa
Everybody / Everyone	Kolhom/ kol had / el-kol
Although	Raghm/raghm annu/pourtant
To feel	Yhess
Past	Madhi
Next (following, after)	Ejey
To like	Yheb / ye'ijeb
In front	Koddem
Next (near, close)	Bahdha / b'jnab
Behind	W'ra
Well	Labes
Goodbye	Bye/ bislema
Restaurant	Mat'aam/resto/restaurant
Bathroom	Salle de bain/toilette/beet el-banu

I don't want to wish you anything bad
Ena ma nhebesh nitmanelek ay shay khayeb
I must forget everybody from my past to feel well
Lezemni nensa kol had min el-madhi mte'i besh nhes labes
I am next to the person behind you
Ena b'jnab eshakhs li w'rak
There is a great person in front of me
Famma shakhs heyel koddemi
I say goodbye to my friends
Ena nkool bislema l's'habee
Where is the bathroom in the restaurant?
Ween e-toilette fil resto?
She has to get a car before the next year
Lezemha tekhu karhba kbal 'am ejjey
I like the house, but it is very small
E'ijbetni el dar, ama hiya sgheera barsha

Bahdha literally means "side." In Tunisian Arabic, it refers to "next." *Bahdheya* is "besides me" and *bahdhek* is "besides you."
*There are three forms of the word "restaurant" / *mat'aam, resto,* and *restaurant* (in French).
*There are two forms of the word "although" / *raghm, raghm annu,* and *pourtant* (in French).
*There are three forms of the word "bathroom" / *salle de bain* (in French, and most commonly used), *toilette, beet el-banu.*

To remove / to take out	Ynahhi
Please	Y'ayshek/min fadhlek/ billehi/ta'mel mzeyya
Beautiful	(M)Mizyein, (F)mizyeina
To lift	Yhez
Include / Including	Bima fi dhelek / b'ei'tibar
Belong	Tebaa'/ mte'
To hold	Yshed/yhez
To check	Yet'aked/ ythabbet
Small	Sgheer
Real	Hakiki/ berrsmi
Weather	Jom'aa/ osboo'
Size	Kobr/ hajm
High	Irtifa'
Doesn't	Moosh
So (as in then)	Yaa'ni
So (as in very)	Barsha / yecer (please read footnote below)
Price	Soom / prix (in French)
Correct	S'heeh

She wants to remove this door please
T'heb tnahhi hedha el-beb y'ayshek
This doesn't belong here, I need to check again
Hedhi moosh teb'aa l'hooni, lezemni nthabet marra okhra
This week the weather was very beautiful
Hal jom'aa taks kein mizyein barsha
I need to know which is the real diamond
Lezemni naa'ref ama hiya el-jawhara el-hakikiya
We need to check the size of the house
Lezemna nthabtu fi kobr el-dar
I want to lift this, so you need to hold it high
Nheb nhez hedhi, donc lezmek t'shed'ha lfook
I can pay this even though that the price is expensive
Najjem nedfaa' hak'ha pourtant soom ghali
Including everything is this price correct?
B'ei'tibar kol-shay, el-prix s'heeh?

*The word "so" translates into *barsha / yecer* and, unlike in English, it is placed after the adjective.

Countries of the Middle East
Bildan el-sharq el-awsatt

Lebanon	Lobnen
Syria	Soorya
Jordan	L'ordon
Israel/Palestine	Isra'eel / filasteen
Iraq	El-Irak
Saudi Arabia	Sa'odiyya
Kuwait	El-Kweit
Qatar	Qatar
Bahrain	El-Bahrein
United Arab Emirates	El-emarat
Oman	'Oman
Yemen	El-Yaman
Egypt	Masr
Libya	Leebya
Tunisia	Tunes
Algeria	Dzzeyir
Morocco	El-Maghreb

Months

January	Janvee
February	Fivree
March	Mars
April	Avreel
May	Mei
June	Jwan
July	Jwilya
August	Oot
September	Septembre
October	Octobre
November	Novembre
December	Décembre

Days of the Week

Sunday	Ahad
Monday	Thnein
Tuesday	Tleith
Wednesday	Erb'aa
Thursday	Khmees
Friday	Jem'aa
Saturday	Sabt

Seasons

Spring	Rabee'
Summer	Seif
Autumn	Khreef
Winter	Shta

Cardinal Directions

North	Shameil
South	Janoob
East	Shark
West	Gharb

Colors

Black	(M)Akhal (F)kahla
White	(M)Abyedh (F) Beidha
Gray	(M)Gri (F) gri
Red	(M)Ahmer (F)Hamra
Blue	(M)Azrek(F)Zarka
Yellow	(M)Asfer (F)Safra
Green	(M)Akhder (F)Khadra
Orange	Bortoukali
Purple	Mauve
Brown	(M)Bonni (F)Bonniyya

Numbers

One	Wehid
Two	Thnein
Three	Tletha
Four	Arb'aa
Five	Khamsa
Six	Sitta
Seven	Sab'aa
Eight	Thmanya
Nine	Tis'aa
Ten	'Ashra

Twenty	'Eshreen
Thirty	Tletheen
Forty	Arb'een
Fifty	Khamseen
Sixty	Sitteen
Seventy	Saba'een
Eighty	Thmeneen
Ninety	Tisi'in
Hundred	Miyya
Thousand	Alf
Million	Malyoon

CONCLUSION

Congratulations ! You have completed all the tools needed to master the Tunisian Arabic dialect, and I hope that this has been a valuable learning experience. Now you have sufficient communication skills to be confident enough to embark on a visit to Tunisia, impress your friends, and boost your resume so good luck.

This program is available in other languages as well, and it is my fervent hope that my language learning programs will be used for good, enabling people from all corners of the globe and from all cultures and religions to be able to communicate harmoniously. After memorizing the required three hundred and fifty words, please perform a daily five-minute exercise by creating sentences in your head using these words. This simple exercise will help you grasp conversational communications even more effectively. Also, once you memorize the vocabulary on each page, follow it by using a notecard to cover the words you have just memorized and test yourself and follow that by going back and using this same notecard technique on the pages you studied during the previous days. This repetition technique will assist you in mastering these words in order to provide you with the tools to create your own sentences.

Every day, use this notecard technique on the words that you have just studied.

Everything in life has a catch. The catch here is just consistency. If you just open the book, and after the first few pages of studying the program, you put it down, then you will not gain anything. However, if you consistently dedicate a half hour daily to studying, as well as reviewing what you have learned from previous days, then you will quickly realize why this method is the most effective technique ever created to become conversational in a foreign language. My technique works! For anyone who doubts this technique, all I can say is that it has worked for me and hundreds of others.

NOTE FROM THE AUTHOR

Thank you for your interest in my work. I encourage you to share your overall experience of this book by posting a review. Your review can make a difference! Please feel free to describe how you benefited from my method or provide creative feedback on how I can improve this program. I am constantly seeking ways to enhance the quality of this product, based on personal testimonials and suggestions from individuals like you.

Thanks and best of luck,

Yatir Nitzany

Printed in Great Britain
by Amazon

66012399R00026